YOUR PASSPORT TO
GERMANY

by Nancy Dickmann

CAPSTONE PRESS
a capstone imprint

Published by Capstone Press, an imprint of Capstone
1710 Roe Crest Drive, North Mankato, Minnesota 56003
capstonepub.com

Library of Congress Cataloging-in-Publication Data
Title: Your passport to Germany / by Nancy Dickmann.
Description: North Mankato, Minnesota : Capstone Press, an imprint of
Capstone, [2023] | Series: World passport | Includes bibliographical
references and index. | Audience: Ages 8-11 | Audience: Grades 4-6 |
Summary: "What is it like to live in or visit Germany? What makes
Germany's culture unique? Explore the geography, traditions, and daily
lives of Germans"— Provided by publisher.
Identifiers: LCCN 2022028952 (print) | LCCN 2022028953 (ebook) | ISBN
9781666390063 (hardcover) | ISBN 9781666390018 (paperback) | ISBN
9781666390025 (ebook pdf) | ISBN 9781666390049 (kindle edition)
Subjects: LCSH: Germany—Juvenile literature.
Classification: LCC DD17 .D46 2023 (print) | LCC DD17 (ebook) | DDC
943—dc23/eng/20220629
LC record available at https://lccn.loc.gov/2022028952
LC ebook record available at https://lccn.loc.gov/2022028953

Editorial Credits
Editor: Carrie Sheely; Designer: Elyse White; Media Researcher: Jo Miller;
Production Specialist: Tori Abraham

CONTENTS

Words in **bold** are in the glossary.

CHAPTER ONE

WELCOME TO GERMANY!

A castle stands on a rocky peak. Its towers reach up toward the sky. Sunlight glints off its white walls. The castle is surrounded by mountains. It looks like something from a fairy tale. This is Neuschwanstein Castle in southern Germany. Built in the late 1800s, it is one of Germany's most popular attractions. More than 1 million people visit the castle every year.

Germany is one of the biggest countries in Europe. About 80 million people live there. Germany has beautiful countryside. It also has busy cities and a rich history.

FACT

Neuschwanstein Castle inspired the look of the castle at Disneyland.

MAP OF GERMANY

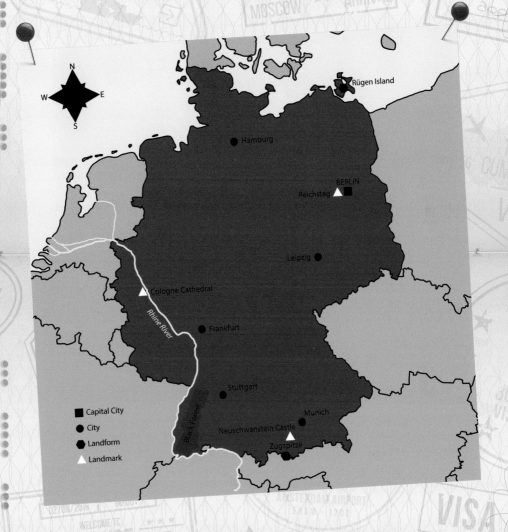

N
W • E
S

Rügen Island

Hamburg

BERLIN
Reichstag ▲ ■

Leipzig

Cologne Cathedral ▲

Rhine River

Frankfurt

Stuttgart

Black Forest

Munich

Neuschwanstein Castle ▲
Zugspitze

■ Capital City
● City
⬣ Landform
▲ Landmark

Explore Germany's
cities and landmarks.

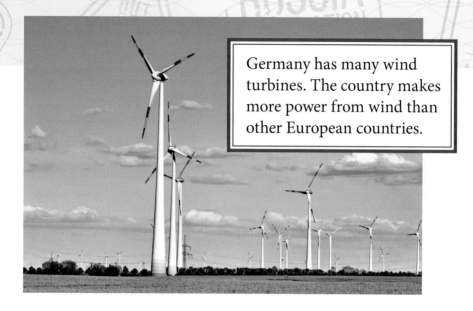

Germany has many wind turbines. The country makes more power from wind than other European countries.

AT THE CENTER OF EUROPE

Germany is in the center of Europe. Travelers and traders have come to Germany for hundreds of years. People from other countries have settled there.

In the 1950s, Germany helped set up the European Union (EU). This is a group of countries in Europe. They work together for peace. They cooperate to boost trade. More countries have joined over the years. Germany is a key member.

Today, the country is a leader in the world. Germany has a strong **economy**. It is a leader in **renewable energy**, including wind power. Germany is known for its high-tech industry.

FACT FILE

OFFICIAL NAME: FEDERAL REPUBLIC OF GERMANY

POPULATION: 83,200,000

LAND AREA: 134,623 SQ. MI. (348,672 SQ KM)

CAPITAL: BERLIN

MONEY: EURO

GOVERNMENT: FEDERAL REPUBLIC

LANGUAGE: GERMAN

GEOGRAPHY: Germany is in north-central Europe. Denmark borders Germany to the north. France, Belgium, Luxembourg, and the Netherlands border Germany to the west. Switzerland and Austria are to the south and southeast, and Poland and Czechia are to the east.

NATURAL RESOURCES: Germany has timber, coal, salt, and natural gas. Farmers raise livestock and grow wheat, barley, sugar beets, and potatoes.

People walk through Marienplatz square in Munich. Many celebrations are held there.

CHAPTER TWO

HISTORY OF GERMANY

People have lived in Germany for a very long time. In a cave, archaeologists found small sculptures. They also found a flute made from animal bone. Scientists believe the flute is more than 35,000 years old!

The bone flute was found in Hohle Fels Cave near Ulm, Germany, in 2008. A team reassembled it from the pieces that were found.

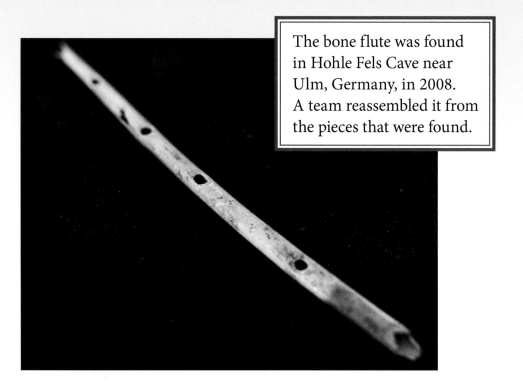

ROMANS AND FRANKS

Many **tribes** have lived in Germany. About 2,000 years ago, some fought against Roman invaders. The Romans never got very far into Germany. A tribe called the Franks became powerful. They pushed the Romans out. In 800, Charles the Great, or Charlemagne, became king. He united many areas under one rule.

Later, Germany was split into different states. Each was ruled by a prince or duke. In 1871, the states formed a single country. It was called the German Empire.

Charles the Great

FACT

In about 1450, German Johannes Gutenberg invented a new kind of printing press. It could produce many copies of a book. Before, they had to be copied out by hand. The printing press meant that books and ideas could be shared like never before.

TWO WARS

Germany fought in World War I (1914–1918) with other countries, including Austria-Hungary and Turkey. These Central Powers fought against the Allies, which included the United States, the United Kingdom, and France. The Central Powers lost the war. After the war, Germany's economy collapsed. Prices for food and other goods went sky-high.

In 1933, Adolf Hitler became the chancellor of Germany. He led the Nazi political party. Hitler said he would help Germany. But he used violence to control people. He led the country into World War II (1939–1945). Millions of people died. This included about 6 million Jewish people that the Nazis killed.

Germany's invasion of Poland started World War II.

TIMELINE OF GERMAN HISTORY

ABOUT 33,000 BCE: Prehistoric people live in what is now Germany.

113 BCE: Germanic tribes first come into contact with the Roman Empire.

9 CE: Germanic tribes win a huge battle with the Romans.

800: Charles the Great is crowned Holy Roman Emperor.

1250: Germany splits into many independent territories.

1871: Many states are united as the German Empire.

1914–1918: The German Empire fights in World War I. After the war, it becomes a republic.

1933: Adolf Hitler becomes leader.

1939–1945: Germany fights in World War II.

1949: Germany is split into East Germany and West Germany.

1990: The two halves reunite into a single country.

2005: Angela Merkel becomes Germany's first female chancellor.

MODERN GERMANY

Germany and the other Axis powers lost World War II against the Allies. In 1949, Germany was split into East Germany and West Germany. The governments of the two sides did not work together. The border between them was closed. Many families were separated. Germans on both sides worked to rebuild their country.

In 1990, Germany reunited. It has been a single country ever since. German leaders now work to make Europe strong. They welcome **immigrants**. Modern Germany is known for its successful businesses.

CHAPTER THREE

EXPLORE GERMANY

Germany is a beautiful country. It has amazing natural areas as well as historic buildings. Nature and history meet along the Rhine. This river flows through western Germany. There are many castles along its steep banks. They are hundreds of years old. Cruise ships take tourists down the river. They admire the unique castles and villages.

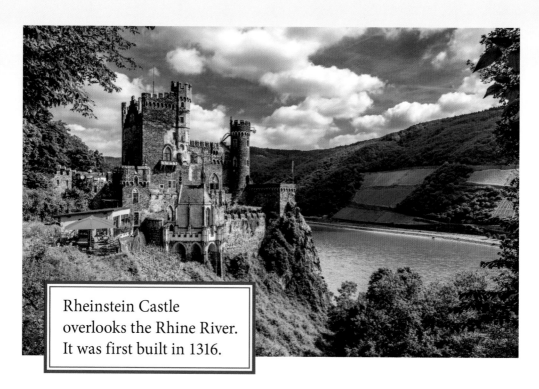

Rheinstein Castle overlooks the Rhine River. It was first built in 1316.

People stroll along the beaches on Rügen Island.

COASTAL AREAS

Most of Germany's rivers flow north. They empty into the North Sea. Germany has two stretches of coastline to the north. The large island of Rügen is on the northeast coast. It has sandy beaches and tall white limestone cliffs. It is a popular place for Germans to spend their summer vacations.

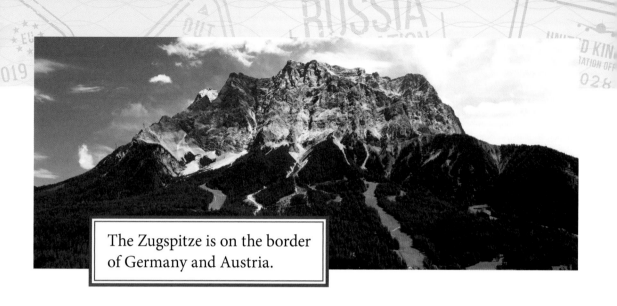

The Zugspitze is on the border of Germany and Austria.

MOUNTAINS AND LAKES

There are mountains in southern Germany. They are part of the Alps. The Zugspitze is Germany's tallest mountain. It is 9,718 feet (2,962 m) tall. There are deep valleys between the mountains. **Glaciers** carved many of them. The area also has many beautiful lakes. Hikers visit the area in the summer. In the winter, skiers take to the slopes.

THE BLACK FOREST

The mountains in the southwest are not as tall. Their slopes are thick with trees. There are waterfalls and hot springs. This is the famous Black Forest. Many of the Grimm Brothers' fairy tales are set there. Wolves, deer, owls, otters, and wild boar live among the trees.

TOWNS AND VILLAGES

Germany has a long history. Many of its towns date back to **medieval** times. They have twisty streets and old wooden buildings. Rothenburg is a town in central Germany. It has many old buildings. Tall houses line the main square. They are painted in bright colors. The town's medieval walls are still standing.

Tourists walk along the streets of Rothenburg.

BUSY CITIES

Berlin is Germany's capital. It is also the country's largest city. The **parliament** meets in a building called the Reichstag. It has a stunning glass dome. The city is known for its arts scene.

Hamburg is a busy port city. It is on the Elbe River near the north coast. Goods from all over the world arrive here. Hamburg has beautiful parks and canals.

Munich is a large city in the far south. Tourists often start there to tour the lakes and mountains. Munich is famous for its museums and restaurants.

Large cargo ships travel in and out of the port of Hamburg. The port is important to the delivery of goods across Europe.

Visitors can climb a spiral ramp to the top of the dome on the Reichstag and watch government leaders at work.

OTHER CITIES

Germany has many large cities. Frankfurt is known for its many banks and skyscrapers. Stuttgart is home to car factories and auto museums. Leipzig has libraries and a historic university.

FACT

The city of Cologne has a grand cathedral. Its twin towers are 515 feet (157 m) tall.

CHAPTER FOUR
DAILY LIFE

Most people in Germany live in cities. Life there is fast-paced and busy. In smaller towns and villages, daily life moves at a slower pace.

People in cities live modern lives. But the past is important, too. Folk music is popular. People keep old **traditions** alive. For example, brides carry a bit of bread and salt at weddings. A myth says that this will bring a good harvest.

SCHOOL

Germany has a strong education system. All children must go to school. In elementary school, the school day lasts about six hours. Most students don't wear uniforms.

Some small German villages are in the country among fields.

Grilled sausages are a popular German food.

FOOD AND DRINK

German meals often include meat and potatoes. Pork is popular, and Germany is famous for sausages. They are called wurst. There are many types. In Berlin, people buy currywurst from food booths. This sausage is served with fries and a spicy sauce.

SAVORY AND SWEET

Stews and other hearty dishes are popular. Thin pieces of meat fried in bread crumbs are called schnitzel. Pasta with cheese sauce and fried onions is another favorite dish. Slow-cooked pot roast is often served with shredded cabbage. Germans also enjoy cakes and sweet treats. To make strudel, people cook apples in a pastry with sugar and cinnamon.

APPLE STRUDEL

The German name for apple strudel is *Apfelstrudel*. This delicious pastry gets its name from German words meaning "apple" and "swirl." Traditional strudel uses a special kind of stretchy dough, but this version uses puff pastry.

Apple Strudel Ingredients:
- 2–3 tart apples
- 1/2 cup raisins (optional)
- 1/4 cup chopped walnuts (optional)
- 1/4 cup brown sugar
- 1 teaspoon cinnamon
- 2-3 tablespoons bread crumbs
- lemon juice
- sheet of ready-made puff pastry
- 1 egg
- 1 tablespoon milk

Apple Strudel Directions:

1. Preheat oven to 350°F.
2. Peel and core the apples. Then cut them into small cubes or thin slices.
3. Mix the apples in a bowl with the raisins and nuts (if using), brown sugar, cinnamon, bread crumbs, and a splash of lemon juice.
4. In a separate bowl, beat the egg with the milk.
5. Unroll the puff pastry on a lightly floured baking sheet. Spread the apple mixture over the middle third of the pastry, leaving an equal-sized area empty on each side.
6. Fold one side of the pastry over the filling and brush it with egg mixture.
7. Fold the other side over and press all the edges together, including the ends.
8. Brush the pastry all over with egg mixture. Cut a few diagonal slits in the top for steam to escape.
9. Bake for 30 minutes or until the pastry is golden brown. Serve in slices with vanilla ice cream.

CHAPTER FIVE

HOLIDAYS AND CELEBRATIONS

Many people in Germany are Christian. Easter is one of the most important holidays. People decorate Easter eggs. They give gifts of paper eggs filled with chocolates. Families go outside to enjoy the spring weather and have egg hunts. They share a meal, which often includes roasted lamb. Dessert is often a cake baked in the shape of a lamb.

People hang colorful eggs on trees outdoors to celebrate Easter.

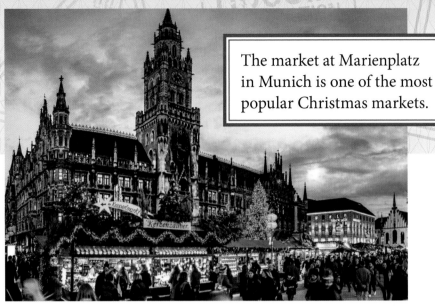

The market at Marienplatz in Munich is one of the most popular Christmas markets.

CHRISTMAS

Christmas is another important holiday. Cities host outdoor Christmas markets. There are people selling gifts and hot food at booths. Christmas trees in the home are a German tradition. They are trimmed with ornaments and lights. On Christmas Eve, families often eat a simple meal of potato salad and sausage. They exchange presents and go to church. On Christmas Day, people often eat roast goose.

FACT

The night before Easter, many people light bonfires. The fires mark the end of winter and the beginning of spring. This is an ancient tradition.

Lit-up rides add to the excitement of Oktoberfest.

CELEBRATING UNITY

German Unity Day is October 3. It remembers the day in 1990 when Germany became a single country again. People get a day off work. Cities host festivals with live music and food booths. Many families celebrate at home or with a picnic.

OLD TRADITIONS

Other celebrations are much older. On April 30, people celebrate Walpurgis Night. They celebrate spring by dressing in costumes and playing pranks. People once believed that witches gathered on Walpurgis Night. They protected themselves by lighting bonfires and making loud noises. They thought this would keep evil spirits away. People still carry on these traditions.

Dancers in leather shorts called lederhosen perform at Oktoberfest.

Oktoberfest happens in Munich in the fall. It lasts more than two weeks. There is plenty of German food. People wear traditional clothes and listen to bands. There are fairground rides, games, and dancing.

CHAPTER SIX

SPORTS AND RECREATION

Soccer is Germany's most popular sport. Many people play soccer for fun. They go to matches to cheer on their favorite teams. Germany's pro league is one of the best in the world. The national teams are very good too. The men's and women's teams have both won the World Cup.

The Germany women's national soccer team won the World Cup in 2007.

Handball is another popular sport. This fast-paced game is played by teams of seven. They pass and throw a ball to score goals.

Car racing is an exciting sport with many fans. Several German drivers have become Formula 1 (F1) world champions.

Many Germans enjoy spending time outdoors. They hike in the beautiful countryside. In winter, many people ski. At the Winter Olympics, Germany does well in sports such as skating and luge.

Hikers can enjoy many scenic views in Germany.

SCHOKOLADENESSEN

This long word means "chocolate eating," and that's what this party game is all about! It's fast-paced and silly.

1. Wrap a chocolate bar in several layers of paper and tie it up with ribbon or string.
2. Put the chocolate on the table with a hat, scarf, mittens, fork, and knife.
3. Sit around the table and take turns rolling a die.
4. When someone rolls a six, they must put on the hat, scarf, and mittens and try to unwrap (and eat) the chocolate using the fork and knife.
5. While they are working, the others continue to roll the die. If someone else rolls a six, the hat and other objects must be passed over.
6. The game continues until all the chocolate is eaten!

ART AND MUSIC

Germany is known for its music. Beethoven and other famous **composers** were born there. Today, orchestras perform across the country. Many people play instruments and sing as a hobby.

Orchestra members tune their instruments before a concert in Hamburg, Germany.

The German government helps fund the arts. It wants everyone to be able to enjoy them. Cities host regular theater and dance performances. There are festivals of film, music, opera, literature, and more. People come from around the world to enjoy the arts.

SOMETHING FOR EVERYONE

Germany is an amazing country full of beauty and history. From mountains to river castles, there is something for everyone to enjoy.

GLOSSARY

composer
(kuhm-POH-zuhr)
a person who writes songs
or music

economy
(i-KAH-nuh-mee)
the ways in which a
country handles its money
and resources

glacier (GLAY-shur)
a large, slow-moving sheet
of ice

immigrant
(IM-uh-gruhnt)
a person who leaves
one country and settles
in another

medieval
(mee-DEE-vuhl)
having to do with the
period of history between
500 and 1450 CE

parliament
(PAR-luh-muhnt)
a group of people who
make laws and run
the government in
some countries

renewable energy
(ri-NOO-uh-buhl
EN-er-jee)
power from sources that
will not be used up, such as
wind, water, and the Sun

tradition
(truh-DISH-uhn)
a custom, idea, or belief
passed down through time

tribe (TRIBE)
a group of people who
share the same language
and way of life